POEMS OF OUR TIME

By the same author:

IN ANOTHER ROOM
THE ENMITY OF NOON

POEMS OF OUR TIME

PETER CHAMPKIN

ROBERT HALE LIMITED

First published in Great Britain 1962

Published by Robert Hale Ltd
63 Old Brompton Road
London S.W.7

Set in Aldine Bembo, and
printed in Great Britain
by Ebenezer Baylis & Son, Ltd.
at the Trinity Press, Worcester

Contents

CONTENTS

CONTENTS

THE HUNTING LODGE

It is, as you may suppose, a slaying
Of animals or something alive
Within one here. The Prince has arranged it,
Being anxious to give.

He is the one we met earlier in dreams,
The organizer of calamity, the man
With equipment for a purpose
To do if he can

Something with weapons and delicate irons
To be mentioned with pride,
As a campaign by a general,
As strength to a bride.

It lies at the end of a lake, being
Of uncertain age, of wood and stone,
A property secluded but inevitable,
Standing alone.

We do not travel as tourists.
I see no sight of exceptional worth,
But tall trees and solemn preparation
For death and birth.

Here the grave huntsmen, peculiar hats,
Disembark, assemble. Follow them.
Now there's a ritual of jollity
Some will condemn

As inappropriate; yet it's a prayer,
I think, a hallowed incantation,
For the Prince will not leave his people
Without salvation.

Horned with high antlers see that house
At the end of a lake, where pines converse
Sadly together. There they make ready,
True to the curse.

* * *

Beyond the lodge inhabited by lonely night
Or hired by men for a night, sleeping,
The woods you hear in lamentation,
You hear them weeping,

And the twittering spirits mourn
In an empty house by the lake again.
Later a bishop will bless the people,
Freed by this pain.

IN GOOD ARRAY

If the ceremonies are interrupted
By explosion or atomic device
The representatives of government must leave first,
Then the Adorable Companies and mace-bearers.

A singular procession it may be,
Some being carried, but no matter,
The leviers of tax shall precede the vulgar,
The local authorities follow in order.

Perfection, obedience and calm,
Simplification of desire
With perfect instruction and obedient example,
A becoming leadership, a civilization.

Day yields to day, life to life
While the management passes, persisting quite.
One who is accountant was junior clerk
And the Chair of Philosophy will not be advertised.

No usual behaviour of cripples,
Extravagant step or doctrine
Should hinder our circuit of the city.
I tell you that the walls will fall.

It was a harlot who survived
With knowledge of a kind, with love.
And the hosts of the Lord ransacked the citadel
Whose righteousness surrounds the world.

A LESSON

The Prince commissioned, where we stand,
A palace, marvellously ornate,
And cunning craftsmen to provide
A watered arrogance beside.

His coming time no prophet told
Or who gave birth. Such omens came.
With light the sun was overcast.
Satan, your evil hope is past.

An old tradition tells the story
How soon a dragon harried us.
The Prince led out his band of freemen
With mortal peril to that demon,

Whence ten horses drew his bulk
For seven leagues, but I digress.
This palace, then encharmed, withstands
The magic of inhuman bands,

And to the Day of Judgment shall
Tower with the Prince's monuments
Of which the shadow has no end.
Thank you. To teach is to pretend.

WHERE IS CASEY?

What has happened to Casey now,
So long after with nothing said?
Did the farm prosper? Do his crops grow?
Are his trees dead?

What has happened to Casey when
Others succeeded, made their mark?
Perhaps he is waiting upon a sign,
Or lies in the dark.

What has happened to Casey who
Wanted support for a new idea,
Always beginning with such as you
A new career?

And where is Casey's home and goal?
Ask empty winds and question then
The universal loving soul.
Amen, amen.

WHAT THE CORPORAL HEARD

An English governess was once employed
To perambulate his sailor-suited children,
And to circumnavigate the villages
Constant in supplying bread, sauerkraut and cheese.

The Count allowed each Christmas time
A holiday more than was customary.
You may be assured that at the inn
His health was drunk. He drank there too.

And there was, I seem to remember, talk
Of conscription then. From the harness works
And county mines men went to the wars
Which, I suppose, were very local affairs.

The brooding Schloss, the ancient name.
They tell such tales, Gefreiter,
When revolution came.

In Wilhelm's time we remember a huge oak
Toppled and fell, and the mark of it
Remains in the stables. Those who were injured
Did lighter work bringing beet from the farms.

The Church remains and some of the outhouses,
And where the Central Medical Unit stands
There was a grotto, quite a surprise for visitors
Who would walk or ride from the railway station.

The brooding Schloss, the ancient name.
They tell such tales, Gefreiter,
When revolution came.

I remember their parasols and she was pretty, his wife—
There's the Centre For Physical Health.
As I was saying—and there, for our Leader,
Is the Monument Of A Thousand Comrades.

The brooding Schloss, the ancient name.
They tell such tales, Gefreiter,
When revolution came.

B

DIFFICULTIES OF COMMUNICATION

(i)

No, I am not a seer; nor do I counsel you,
For who can take advice by word or book?
And barely by example and not by gift;
Living in isolation we cannot understand it.

Thank you, no money. I'm quite well fed
Having sufficient for my single day,
Nor need you cast your clothing off on me
Or secretly arrange for my subsistence.

You give me audience, expecting news
Of novel invention or a plot revealed;
But there is no plot against Your Highness
And the calm spirit need not invent.

O Prince, there is no evil, there is no good,
But such juncture as always has been
With such alternation of extremes
In that devils must pray and angels copulate.

The holy man is silent, for his speech
Says less than has been said. If he should speak
Tumult and anger would engulf the world
Once more in consequence of his love.

And again it must come to that, some Will
Needing an affirmation, wanting the solace
Of being right. But when you address your captains
Omit all reference to this.

DIFFICULTIES OF COMMUNICATION

(ii)

To speak with you coherently, he said
Who answered next, that will be difficult.
First the opinion I remember first,
You cannot grow unless you want to grow.
(This much we understand. It comes from books.)
Next a more complex knowledge, listen now,
Do not become what educators want.
(We grasp this concept. What has he in mind?)
A third injunction follows, single, short:
Become yourself. How excellent that is.
(He echoes ancient Greeks. How excellent.)
Fourthly a novel note: an instrument
Must play the noise you make with it alone.
(Noise well describes this tone. But what is next?)
My fifth a doctrine taught religiously:
Nothing is learnt that is not given first.
(Time passes. Should the commentator sleep?)
Lastly the God incarnate tells me this:
The love of all is purpose, nothing else.
(His purpose seems to falter. Still he speaks.)
The Tao that can be expressed is not the eternal Tao.
The name that can be uttered is not its eternal name.

WAYS OF LOVE

(i)

He calls for music, being so in love,
And being passionate, for Pandarus.
Unmoved above
His birth-star can foretell the wanton fuss

Of quiet intrigue and desperate recourse
With subtler preparation in his hall.
This curious force
Waits like an old toad blinking at her wall.

Only their union now can consummate
Unnatural effort to a natural mark;
And of the fate
That follows kisses nothing shows the dark.

They draw the curtains, so our tale withdraws
From this renowned conspiracy of love.
Now close the doors
But mark those eager cupids carved above.

In different times she lies at his right hand,
A whitened thing, whose limbs as close remain.
In all his land
They celebrate with ritual again

Their mystic marriage and the birth and death
Of dynasties that half a smile can move.
His panting breath
Stays fixed in laughing cupids there above.

WAYS OF LOVE

(ii)

Where are the pictures that you made of me
In bays of night when silver flickered there?
I left them in an attic by that sea,
I lost them when I left you unaware.

And of the crooked growths of other time
Did you keep one to make the record true?
Life's record is too short to be sublime.
It weakens me. Your memory weakens you.

White doves fly out; they never come again.
They pain me afterward, recalled to heart.
I paint them so, and I avoid that pain
That is but art, but transitory art.

Do you feel nothing and forget how then
There was no knowledge to acquire but one?
As wheeling planets, wanderers all men;
This poem is my distance from your sun.

WAYS OF LOVE

(iii)

Fifteen and sixteen,
A sultry September
Standing together, utterly blue their eyes,
And skins of white and strawberries.

Discarded from amber,
Last light of September
Their clothes lay; and one, naked, bent
Her frail bright body and leant

Over her sister
Warm flash of September
Who gave to her firm, gay breasts
Her delicate fingers and kissed,

Then fell on her knees
Fires burn in September
And wildly and suddenly plunged her way
Through all that gold, young hair to the grey

Shadows beneath.
Summer stays in September
Counting on fingers, the other recovers
The dances, the promise, the lovers.

(VERLAINE, *Pensionnaires.*)

WAYS OF LOVE

(iv)

Rage, dark figures, rage!
Rise, ancient kings, and fight!
On the borders of our space
Night is at war with night.

There's honey in the earth
But never sweet for man.
Lady, can you allay
The fever you began?

All life is love at war.
How shall the body rest,
When striving things that are
In love are happiest?

WAYS OF LOVE

(v)

As amorous still, as young, she says,
"One lover you consorted with
Before your birth. We parted then.
You loved me once; but twice I lie with men."

The place around that bed is cold,
The great world spins, but who shall mind,
Hearing her whisper in such mirth,
"Love me again, possess the lovely earth."?

A ROUND TRIP

(i)

Accoutred well, he leads beyond
The rugged Alps a noble train.
They tread that glittering carpet now,
The Tuscan plain.

Those cities, burnished with such art,
The Prince must pause to marvel at.
Venus has voyaged here, and here
Lorenzo sat.

Scholars and poets, artisans
Renew his tired thought and sing
How Nature, too long barbarous,
Yields everything.

Following east his retinue
Stoned portraiture in gold displays;
Then seas caress his gift-filled ship,
His great sails blaze.

The cities of another plain
Ruined, behold his passage there.
He ponders on the meaning of
Their proud despair.

These bright entablatures relate
That finish here with his return,
Magnificence must yield to fate
And towers burn.

The wonders of a wider world
Others, unborn, will search and mark
Who follow after this grave Prince
And find the dark.

A ROUND TRIP

(ii)

Equator Lines for the Orinoco
Announce a cruise for a hundred strong.
There will be gin and rum and cocoa
And music and sunshine all day long.

Equator Lines for the Rio Grande
Arrange all travel by land and sea.
They have a personal scheme in hand
For a vacation in Arcady.

Equator Lines have trained and sent
Agents to every country and isle.
The colour in their advertisement
Is blue as Tahiti, green as the Nile.

Equator Lines have an expert staff
To find without fuss your destination,
Where you can love or swim or laugh
Or mix with others of equal station.

Who mourns above us, having sent
His son to sacrifice; assigns
The chartered earth and firmament
To hire at Equator Lines?

A ROUND TRIP

(iii)

Now the rare phial, the interesting cure,
The final potion, last beatitude.
It was a long and well conducted tour
And showed us much. The commentary was good.

This is the distillation; let us drink.
I hope we may resolve experience
Of sights and sounds. It's time, I think,
To try with chemistry the total sense.

Come close to me. I do remember just
A fellow gave a sermon upon God,
And once a woman so inflamed my lust . . .
And I recall a book my teacher read.

Something should come of this—to see life whole
At this last meeting. There are pictures now
Of that grim war. I never killed a soul
And have two children and observed the law.

THE THEME OF HAMELIN

(i)

Little town, he was seen last
Who took your children, counselling a king.
Another country, far away, received them.

Still you shed passionate tears,
Wives of aldermen, and execrate his name,
But lack of magic lost your children's love.

For what had you to give
But gloomy prenticeships and solemn robes
To all their restless beauty, called it care?

They broke your barriers, citizens,
And passed forever, following him once,
And are grown into different people.

* * *

If a feast was wanted
Or statue in your counting-house of gold
Or an immediate prayer against the plague,

Money provided it
From central authority, but now, citizens,
There is much more to be acquired

Than quiet careers or many books.
Nothing you read treats of this fortitude,
Not the whole civic library.

THE THEME OF HAMELIN

(ii)

And the Council for Medical Bereavement
agree? Yes, and the Association
for Higher Education, and the Committee
of Clear Mind and Thought. They all agree.

And the Executioner shall be termed Executor.
Yes; dry, if you please, and just a trace of water.
Has Johann Silbermund been briefed?

Conscripted fathers, I arise to urge
a single law to purify the race.
How many children grow to spread disease,
soreness in body, sickness of the mind,
live to contaminate the world and lack,
above all else, responsibility . . . ?

Alas, when learned senators expound
their syllogisms dropping on the ground,
my children, it is time to end your play;
I know another place and far away.

INTELLIGENCE FROM THE FIELD

(i)

This is the history of what I know.
There were, High Prince, opposing factions,
Myself conscripted upon one of them,
Willing to do as any man must

Or more to acquire a special award.
First, cutlass-drill and intricate formation,
Then with general explosive
The study of particular effect.

I shall not describe a period in which
Gestures and oratory were practised,
And importunement and a sexual skill.
Now it became our turn in the ranks

To persuade the enemy to yield to us.
They, with as strong intention, urged
We join with them. The side enlisting me
Was less successful at the start,

Left many prisoners, some of whom survive.
At length my Duke's men, better allied now,
Prevailed and on a monument declared
The Margravine obsessed. I think she was.

And now our prison has a different name,
Food is altogether better and one can wash
More frequently. Some think that after a while
We may look for further release

And true ablution in those extensive waters
Flowing into our time and beyond.
Prince, once I was young and earnest
And fortunate and full of fine beliefs.

INTELLIGENCE FROM THE FIELD

(ii)

Attack him with a spear
Or heave a stone at him; then tear
Out of his ribs his gory heart
And then devour that lovely part.

Bring him back alive
And stage a circus. After five
The children may return to tea
And chatter of the chimpanzee.

Put him in a shop
And hang his quartered limbs to drop
Their blood on tickets with a price.
A leg of him is very nice.

And there are other tricks
To blow apart or to transfix
What lives; and I have heard it said,
'Count no man fortunate but dead.'

Good soldiers aim to kill
The enemies who do them ill,
And generals contemplate the mess.
Cet animal est méchant? Yes.

INTELLIGENCE FROM THE FIELD

(iii)

Around about Kalyma
A dreadful thing took place.
—I do not understand your words
And do not know your face.

—Kalyma is a wooded hill
On which tall fir trees grow.
But cut them, others come from seed
And still the fir trees show.

—You speak, a foreign traveller,
In words I cannot sound,
And point from Nature's living things
To dead things underground.

—Kalyma's hill was quite fenced in.
A nation carried there
Perpetual heaviness and sin,
Continual despair.

—Where have you come from, lunatic
With hopeless, gesturing hand?
Your mortal sounds, disharmonies
I cannot understand.

—Around about Kalyma
A dreadful thing took place,
For there is no one left to speak
The language of my race.

APPOINTMENTS

(i)

It is time to appoint the officers,
Some for the great charitable trusts
And some for cultural and traffic problems;
There shall be higher officers to co-ordinate them.

And the Mother of God requires an officer
To minister in the chapel;
And certainly the officers in the treasury
Must be unimpeachable.

There shall be officers of law
To register liaisons decently
And officers to disapprove indecency
Wherever it is practised.

A Central Office shall establish
A national registry of officers,
Or *tabula custodum plebis*,
With power to determine increments.

These being appointed shall appoint others,
Bringing about a constitutional society
That the immutable laws of Locke
May be justified with officers.

Within this framework cars may come and go,
Coffee be taken, dry martinis drunk;
And there will be officers looking downward
At the very last.

APPOINTMENTS

(ii)

O eminent lecturers,
givers of educational advice,
administrative women, teachers in the field, chairmen
and especially sociological experts,
researchers in anthropology, economics, history,
authorities on Africa or racial issues
and, I begin to think, archaeologists,
pray enter into long silence,
for your work is completed,
your Institutes self-perpetuating;
your sound is gone out into all lands.

IN THE NAME OF GOD

I overlook the blossoming of trees,
Each handsome flower and the austere vineyard,
See anxious animals persist, renew themselves
And the long occupation of the spider
And what the sea holds; learning by these.

Looking upon what I have created,
Man and everything that moves on land,
In stream and ocean, great things in space,
My one experience cannot comprehend it.
Live, little children, and inform me more.

As one increases I grow surely there,
Earnestly seeking. If our ascertainment
Discovers no mystery then I must remain
The High Inscrutable, never adore my works
Or the operation of man and woman.

In his exalted choice my will expands,
And laughing then, my spirit knows that glee;
In loving his children I become his father,
Calling me God, I worship him alone
And his life is the scope of my understanding.

And the idiot may increase my experience
But the confident man will not allay me.
Women, who bear and preserve my tuition,
Do not forsake or leave me barren of hope
For I want to understand much, to explain.

CLEAR CONVERSATION

No, Jack, let others be kind to the poor.
The rich, if they want, can be kind to me.
—But haven't we met somewhere before?
Long time no see.

Well, for a while I worried my head,
Went where the trains and the bowlers go.
Wasn't it better than being dead?
—My answer's no.

Then came the war when we thought it true
The more we suffered, the better might be
The place today. We saw it through.
Long time no see.

First I voted with this crowd, then that,
Though what they said didn't make it so.
I've an automobile and a special hat . . .
—My answer's no.

I tried to be one of the men who show
Judgement, bearing, authority.
—They sold me down river a while ago.
—Long time no see.

And what do you do that signifies?
—Do what I think and I think slow.
—And won't you work for the wiser guys?
—My answer's no.

All right, one more if you let me pay,
And you have one, so make it three.
—I'll go with you, Aussie, all the way;
Long time no see.

AN INTERRUPTION

But what is that? And who is there?
Who knocks upon the door?
Is it a stranger whom I fear?
The stranger knocked before.

Is he a friend or friend in need
Of friendship, seeking you?
It is the enemy of love
And this is true.

But let me leave you, for I know
That you will speak alone.
Ah, do not leave me! Touch my flesh
And ice-cold bone.

How shall I stay? He knocks again,
The earth shakes and the post.
O Saviour on the cross of pain!
O Holy Ghost!

Fear is such failing. Without fear,
With friendship let him in.
O grim Redeemer of the world!
O price of sin!

A PASSING FAVOUR

If you'd point your camera here, Sir,
And connect your microphones,
I should say—but do not fear, Sir,
A simple man among his bones—

If you'd ask my life and story,
The kingdoms I have known and thrones,
The disappointments and the glory
Of one lying with his bones,

If you'd kindly interview me,
Speak with me in undertones,
Give the deference that's due me
As I lie among my bones,

If you'd gone where I have been, Sir,
If you'd heard the shouts and groans,
If you'd seen what I have seen, Sir,
Here reclining with my bones,

If you'd listen to the teacher,
If you'd read these curious stones,
You would know that every creature
Stays in silence with his bones.

JUBILATION DAY

On jubilation day the silly sun arose.
We rise exulting on this day of days,

And in the market-place we stand about
The public monument, our clothing neat.

One of the leaders usually speaks first;
The leader of the leaders follows last.

Yet waiting from the dawn to half past nine,
No news has been received and nothing seen,

Although this day is registered as one
When we commemorate what first began;

And we must be reminded what it was
By someone wise and good and full of phrase.

Let us rejoice immediately with cause
Unclarified. There must be power and laws.

A LOST WORLD

(i)

A feast shall be given in the Prince's name
For squires and burghers, for us all.
What preparation and business
With carpenters and caterers!

A velvet canopy is spread
Aloft on poles, enriched with gold,
A marvellous excitement
For peasant and craftsman.

At noon a holy service shall
In God's great name be solemnized.
Your most respectable clothing,
Your fussiest hat!

Then at the river gorgeous rites;
Wrestling and games shall follow them.
But let us go to the river now
To see the fat men.

With murmurous evening Hesper brings
Such jollity, such rest to toil.
But what explodes in the sky
And then such silence?

A LOST WORLD

(ii)

Those trains, expanding on the English land,
After Royal Oak
none can remember. Some ghost of middle class,
if he should seek
the old speech and dust of Harrow Road,
cobbled, mid-week,
his growing up forgotten, now returning
would speak

of glazed brick, wire bells, same doors
ever repeating,
'Clutch my polished esteem.' He clutches his heart.
He knew of this meeting
in lands removed, unknown in this squalor,
less exciting
than the forms, the ragged face he recalls,

with ales advertised still; porter has gone, and here
inspection invited
somewhere. Now accepting their meaning with those
so long seated
by the piping of bars, in plush corners where
glances are mated,
he forgets, is forgotten, but cannot be different.

From buses emerges at noon
a desperate hurry
from vegetable gutter to gutter, crossing here
with a basket of worry
to rush to a frying of chips
for Tom, Harry,
to heave at some terrible door, weary.

Between Heaven and Harrow there's work
in a store
for a woman, or cleaning a stair in Westbourne Grove,
where the star
or mortality sets, and the bus stops by request
from afar,
and the scroll of Imperial Stout unfolds.

THE HEAVENS SURVEYED

Of course he's culpable. To promulgate such laws
To save, maintain our rights, he asks our Christian names,
The date and origin of birth and how we live.
Why pay bald-headed bureaucrats for this?
Enlisted dogs, what is our pedigree?

In my case what befell? I bring a proper suit
Against a petty trader known to all of you;
The thing drags on while blatant fraud supplies
Diluted milk, adulterated bread,
Diluted wine from an adulterer!

And more abuse; listen, who has the proper right
To use what public guilders bought, the parks I mean
And the arena? Who but our sort, gentlemen?
There'll be hard questions in the Presence Room
With harder knocking on some reverent pates.

Then comes inflation. Stuff bought yesterday at this,
Money invested then, and what's our profit now
Except this paper money and a heap of more?
Trust in the Rathaus, trust the councillors
But be most certain that the poor will pay.

My people hear my voice. I strive to be
Your governor under God. The doubt strikes here.
Am I the Christ come to deliver you?
You made me Prince, now cynic of your ways.
Why do you need me? It is I need you.

ANSWERS IN THE DARK

(i)

Say what you will, whatever you think first.
Our diagnosis rests on evidence
You must surprise us with, adventurer.

What does he do but go into a house
Of *bona robas*, the man of justice? What
Is his thought but pleasure well enrobed?

What does he speak but amicable words,
The public figure? He is the friend in need,
Needing the wretched for environment.

What does he teach but questionable truth,
The teacher, framing questions with an art
That who can answer them stay ignorant?

How does he grow, the child who grows with you
Into yourself, successful *entrepreneur*?
A satisfying process before sleep.

I see the discoverer, the artist, the lover,
The bold man searching the land, the son of man
Never discovered, tormented on a couch.

ANSWERS IN THE DARK

(ii)

Nothing that wandering sunlight brings
Or flying wings, all white, can sweep,
Not all the wilderness of sleep,

No calm that voice and music sings,
No happy notion of the mind
Can treat the sorrow of our kind

From infancy, when we transgressed
His ukases, stern lines of doom.
Father and Sire, thy kingdom come.

If that affliction could be less,
If innocence could quite extend,
I should not need your laughter, friend.

ANSWERS IN THE DARK

(iii)

If it's love you wait upon
When life and anger meet,
Know such company has gone,
You walk an empty street.
Be careful in your solemn ways
Lest the loneliness of days
Be sweet.

If some rest you think is yours
When the hubbub's over,
Know that by established laws
Nothing can recover
Breath that whispered childish things,
Hope a lover sent on wings
To lover.

If it's purpose that you want
When position fails,
Know the bitterness they meant
Whose purpose fixed with nails
Intending man upon a tree,
Such hate, O holy mystery,
Prevails.

TO THE EDITOR

Sir, Having been for certain years
Seconded Researcher in Ultima Thule,
I have a modicum of experience
And knowledge of the wandering tribes.

These range the land. There is no certain view
Or document of their combined opinion,
For some who barely walk upright
Have scarcely learned to think.

But for the impossible distances,
The space where natural life abounds,
The Phagomani would be docile now
And ready for the tape recorder.

The timid Ammonese, now rare,
Exist alone in dwindling numbers
Herding their flocks; but barely they
Have learned to populate themselves.

Here I have never seen a sinciput,
Homunculus or any sentient thing
That could discriminate itself from these.
In consequence I note a general peace.

A SEQUENCE OF DAYS

(i)

How kindly were the faces looking in
That splendid house with figures on the lawn.
Gently and easily the fountains splashed
Where he was born.

This archtype of all glory stayed with him
In adolescence, if he ever grew;
Old-fashioned, you would say, meticulous
And pious, too,

And giving much away, regretting much.
Whose character is this that I display?
The Prince's own. Now have another drink
To yesterday.

But there's a devil in him somewhere; see
How he eludes the processes of pain!
Yet suffers all things all mutations bring
And lives again

In every man, in every grave discourse
Brought by philosophy upon his woe,
So powerful is the providence that armed
Him long ago.

A SEQUENCE OF DAYS

(ii)

Inglassed in celadon,
They make a servant of his tongue,
They glitter with the young and strong,
Theirs is such porcelain.

Entwined in chord and verse,
They bring the measures of their ease,
To him uncursed with hope or cares,
They make such poetry.

Look, they have built a wall
Against the battery of ill
And manned the fortress of one will,
His blood and family!

With present sense and hand
They stem the onslaught of his kind,
They build the mansion of one mind,
His willing skill.

How does he name that part
Of life that lacerates the heart
And fevers passion with its heat?
A salary, a slavery.

D

A SEQUENCE OF DAYS

(iii)

Winds tear about and there are sighs; the house,
Edged on the rocks, resists each gust yet shakes.
The great seas crash upon each seeking cape.

What then will be destroyed? What loneliness
At nightfall come upon an empty room?
One travels here. He shall not come by sea.

By typed correspondence from an actuary,
A strange official writing proper words,
The fact will be advised most certainly.

And the familiar postman will deliver it
Being involved in all excess of news.
If God exists he learns much in this way.

Nothing will be torn from his register
And no statistic be reduced by one.
That ancient spirit, man's long self renews him.

By this vicissitude his thoughts grow wise,
Each crack of circumstance informs him more.
Sleep, now, and rest. He must have interval.

THE SOLITARY PART

Long after the poet has gone
His songs remain in the streets,
In the voices of autumn,
In the noise of vagabonds.

Adventurer, he finds no friend
Or parliament beneath the sun.
His speech is suddenly heard
In a cry, in a word
Long after the poet has gone.

THE GOLDEN BALL

. . . I toss the golden ball to you
—NIETZSCHE

It is your turn upon the spoken cue
To go to school in tricks and liberal arts
And vie with others, desperate as you,
For an award of excellence in parts.

The stage is set to test integrity
Of purpose and the management of men.
Now act your best tonight, so let there be
Light and some trumpets and your gestures then.

That scene went well: the eminent in books
Wait in the wings, you took the audience so,
And by your bearing and your clever looks
Showed where the ways of education go.

But here an interval. There's no acclaim
While the young actor changes cloak and mask.
A time disturbs the charity of fame.
Why does the goddess hesitate? you ask.

The truth is she's a strumpet. I'd speak too
About your worthy motives if you'd let
Me think. That's something there's no time to do.
But never mind, we shall succeed as yet

Or shall we? It seems you're ageing fast to us.
Your last appearance wasn't quite the same.
Banking? Detergents? What a lifetime's fuss!
The play's no good. The author gets the blame.

NIGHT CLEARS

It was a ragged man
Stood up, apostrophized the dawn,
Insane, awry. And when I saw his face
The great sun came to burst upon that place.

Before that day began,
Before that darkness was so torn,
His crazed ambition was to understand
The slow intention, the high blazing land.

SAYINGS OF THE PRINCE

He gave out little, as this age pretends,
And less important was his mien and poise
Than his companions', busy at their ends,
Fermenting occupation with a noise.

They heard him say, it was the harvest season,
He never spoke of conduct or of art,
The toothsome apple has sufficient reason,
It has no need of justice in its heart.

And one replied, it was a bouncing fellow,
Here is no parallel of any sort;
Its life is short, insentiate; being mellow,
It is consumed or rots away in dirt.

He gave out little, as this age pretends,
And less important was his mien and poise
Than his companions', busy at their ends,
Fermenting occupation with a noise.

A CIVIC RECEPTION

Highness, a welcome. Much will pass and change.
This customary meeting stands
Unaltered by vicissitude
In foreign lands.

Our fortunes multiply, our stocks increase
With cosiness and warmth in living.
All this with you we celebrate
In royal thanksgiving.

Old men are grateful, for they rest secure;
Youth has ambition, well it may
With profits shared, long holidays
And proper pay.

Our newer buildings, well designed and large,
Befit our citizens who thrive
Upon the business of the nation
From nine to five.

I know the dungeons in your citadel,
Ominous ravens in your tower,
How darkness generates with lust
No flower, no flower.

THE LORD OF TASTE

We saw in the Uffici how his gaze,
Obsessed with resurrection, blinded sight;
And how his mind, incomparably old,
Renewed our thought.

We read in his great book an epic tale
Of which the tragedy was present truth,
Learned his damnations to avert our own,
Clutching his text.

We heard his music pounding at the wall
Of sense, wherever strangers lay asleep,
And woke to all things in such symphony
Quiet or turbulent.

We saw the artistry in all his view,
Bringing to art such excellent debate.
Now let him come, and we, compose ourselves
Toward a master.

Sirs, greeting. I am good Sir Tenement
In whom you live and furnish your home well.
Be quite at ease with me; I come once more
Collecting rents.

A CHAPTER OF HISTORY

After the swearing in
Incomparable emotion holds the crowd.
'At this solemn moment,' says the commentator,
'All hearts and minds are with the Prince.'

He with a noble mien,
Gravamen becoming to his rank
And magnificence, mounts the rostrum
'With dignity,' says the loudspeaker.

I have never been present
With such a multitude as this, nor can hope
Again to see such greatness gathered,
So fateful an occasion.

And in space are portents
Of eclipse and unusual motion. Great stars
Are moved. The brochure calls it
'The noblest sight in Christendom.'

Being with circumstance preoccupied,
Having seen rank fall to rank
And classes change, I find I have forgotten
The date and nature of the activity.

IN THE FALL

(i)

Reading in the autumn woods I renounce
The wisdom taught me, impartment of books.
Busy with ritual, my daughter
Arranges dolls on the grass.

One sage is concerned with behaviour,
Another, the duties of an upright man.
Having been myself all my days,
It would be sinful to repent.

No noise the river makes can stir
The branches of a rooted tree.
Your altercations far away
Cannot distract my silence.

IN THE FALL

(ii)

Throughout this hour a wind is stirring
My old trees, their blossom gone.
Children who play in the orchard
Nourish the garden. I hear

Children with children, laughing, singing,
Swinging high into the leaves;
They always surprise the garden,
They never finish their song.

From generation the generation
Know the unknowable, five years old.
Children who cannot remember
Grow to be husband and wife.

When sons and daughters find their lovers
In their high summers, their autumn falls.
Children who understand sunlight,
Older, wake to oblivion.

Night is a history; under its darkness
Day delivers voice upon voice.
I hear you singing in the orchard
Children who cannot remember.

TO AN OVERLORD

Pray disregard the ancient speech,
Give small attention to the creed.
Wisdom and faith we do not need.

The heavens that we cannot reach
May desolate our lives and earth.
But there's a fixity at birth

That nothing you can do or say
Is as significant by far
As *Justify the thing you are,*
Welcome this stranger every day.

IN EARLY MORNING

The bright stars give you light,
The slow moon climbs around you.
My daughter of the night,
What harmonies surround you!

From distances of sleep
Your slow-eyed beauty waking
Looks back into the deep,
What leaving, what forsaking?

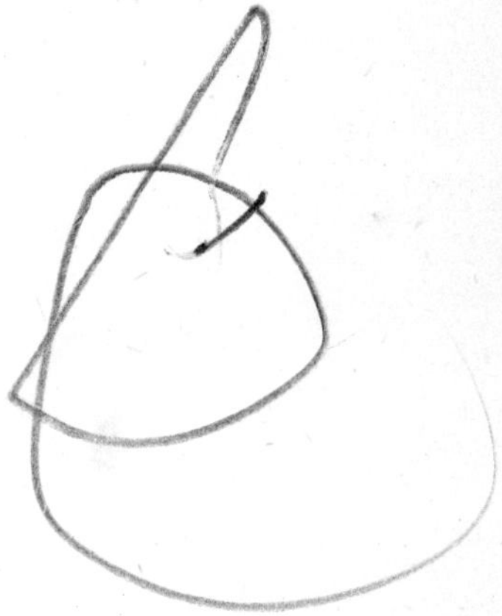